What readers are saying about *Meandering Mindfulness*

"Chrystine Julian approaches varied topics with courage and finesse, aspects fitting of a great poet. She defends the freedoms we love and champions some extraordinary ones, too. Every page is accessible and clear as she challenges us to develop our own intuitions and insights. My advice is to try it on, read, and then look in the mirror. Chances are, you won't see yourself in quite the same way."

Nancy Krieg — American poet and musician

"Chrystine Julian's poems carve out a space for themselves...one surprising slice at a time. Even the short pieces are mighty in meaning and insight. From the very few lines that embody a world view of trees to the vulnerability of passion and love, Chrystine manages to touch the heart, and intrigue the mind. I highly recommend her lovely book of poetry, *Meandering Mindfulness.*"

Ruth Light — Women's National Book Association

"Chrystine Julian is a unique and personal voice. Her keen eye and ear give lyrical expression to the most ordinary occurrences of life, and her imagination transforms them from the mundane to the magical. In turn she finds in the unusual and extraordinary simplicities that make these events accessible to everyday human understanding."

John Bragin — Core Faculty Member,
UCLA Human Complex Systems Program

Also by Chrystine Julian

Sensual Spirit...poetry and thoughts from the place where body and soul meet

"What a rapturous book! Chrystine Julian weds wit and wisdom, body and spirit, in these poems. Her warmth and humor and deep insight radiate off every page."
Gayle Brandeis, author of "Fruitflesh, Seeds of Inspiration for Women that Write," "Self Storage" and the Bellwether Prize winner, "The Book of Dead Birds"

"Chrystine Julian is an amazing modern day poet seer."
The Wellness Times

"Wonderful. I like the passion... its lushness."
Eric Ashford - UK contemporary mystic poet

"I read the first two or three poetry writings from your book today.... WOW! Such magic in how you write! It is transforming."
Rachel Forsyth - Laughter Yoga Instructor

Long Tongue Love - improvisational percussion
Available on CD and digital download

By
Chrystine Julian

Edited by
Ina Hillebrandt

Meandering Mindfulness
Poems from the place where wander and wonder merge

By Chrystine Julian

Edited by Ina Hillebrandt
Cover art, cover and interior design by Chrystine Julian

Published by Pawpress
Brentwood Village • PO Box 492213
Los Angeles, CA 90049
E-mail: annap@InasPawprints.com

Library of Congress Catalog-in-Publication Data
Julian, Chrystine, 1953-
  Meandering mindfulness : poetry from the place where wander and wonder merge / by
Chrystine Julian ; [edited by Ina Hillebrandt].
     p. cm.
  ISBN 978-1-880882-13-9 (alk. paper)
  I. Hillebrandt, Ina, 1943- II. Title.
  PS3610.U534M43 2009
  811'.6--dc22
                        2009012881

a **Pawpress** Book

Printed in the United States of America by Lightning Source, on acid-free paper, from pulp of non-endangered species, non-old growth trees.

Meandering Mindfulness

Poetry from the place where
wander and wonder merge

By
Chrystine Julian

Foreword

It has been my absolute privilege to once again work with Chrystine Julian. Her new book, *Meandering Mindfulness,* with its alternately delicate, bawdy, deeply sensual, insightful, politically astute and "silly" writings, challenges, entertains and leaves me always wanting more.

Ina Hillebrandt, Editor and Publisher

Dedication

This collection is dedicated to all of the great teachers in my life: the ones that cut me off in traffic, ignore and/or use me, and all of the others that have shown me how to love when loving isn't easy.

Thank you!

Introduction

I often wonder while wandering. In fact my greatest pleasure from travel is derived from the manner by which it forces my mind to consider, visualize and value new and old things. I am learning to be present, conscious, and mindful regardless or in response to whatever geography surrounds me. It is a process in which I am being educated in freedom, unbound from memory, while not being indentured to a future.

I love the way wander and wonder play off each other along with the images derived from their transposition. Often my body questions the stresses and demands while my mind travels beyond circumstance and drifts about the landscapes of contemplation and mind conceived realities.

A river meanders based on forces of mass, gravity and geology. In a similar fashion the poems in this collection flow in accordance with large, unseen restrictions and energies. This is not a travel log but rather a scrapbook of thoughts snapped in tourist fashion.

I am hopeful that you will enjoy the slideshow and be inspired to wander about mindfully on your own as the opportunity is presented to you.

Chrystine Julian

TABLE OF CONTENTS

She

Messiah Girl Melissa

Messiah girl Melissa came to this place with love.
She walked through villages of the philosophical poor.
The world refused to pay attention because there was no budget for
her ideas.
Perhaps it was just a girl thing.

She exposed her heart but not her flesh.
Miracles are no match for media marvels.
In an urban desert she tried to rise through days of trial.
This savior girl was tempted and victorious but still unnoticed.

She taught the thought that temporal beauty is transient at best and
frequently pretty stupid.
Was messiah girl ignored because she kept her radiance so neatly
tucked in?
Would enlightened boy Bob have the same problem?
She surrendered to obscurity then took a new name and
occupation.

She may live near you, but you will never know because you didn't
notice when she did.

She is Different

She is different,
bare footed in a booted crowd.
She wears flowing skirts
in a straight suited paradigm.

I saw her again yesterday.
Her gossamer scarf
played with the wind.
She walked. I imagined.

In a vegetarian world
She is a can of Spam.
On a stage of theocracy
her part is heresy.

In a play thing
of square pegs
and round holes
she is the oval one.

She is consistent.
She does her bit
by never being
the one that fits.

But she expects
respect for diligence
and dedication
to her undiluted truth.

Chrystine Julian

Her neck stretches tight
to push her head high.
Her shoulders are wide
with pride and strength.

She stands lean and tall,
a statement of being,
as if she is one finger raised
in the middle of a fist.

Hers is a designer life,
with spirit immaculate,
conceived and constructed
by individual conception.

I watch from a distance
and smile at her style
of dress and addressing
the rest of the world.

No one else notices.
Perhaps she is an object
of imagination, stimulation
or per chance,

just my projection.

Morning Queen Regime Change

Some call her homeless, but…

On an early morning walk she owns the world.
The yellow daisies drinking from the sprinkler,
The broad but empty boulevard,
The whole length and breadth of city lights
Sparkling in a special treasure chest
Opened before her hill top throne.
All is hers alone.

Suddenly a flickering seer of sun creeps
From his hiding beneath the eastern horizon,
Foretelling that this sovereign will soon be toppled,
And her kindly kingdom repossessed at the hands
Of hoards of horns and unlit headlights with
No respect for sprawling predawn splendor,
As her royalty is undone.

She acquiesces to retreat from the street,
Allow the would-be rulers to arise from rest, lay ruin
And pillage a pauper's paradise with no regard
For the value of what they have raped and
Trampled in their brief and temporary triumph.
Yet she knows no regrets as she has
A perfectly plotted plan.

Before another morning comes,
She will ascend and reign again.

Chrystine Julian

Date Night

There are no metaphors here.
This is my reality so I'll tell it
as straight and clear as I can and
you need to listen, very carefully.
I enjoy the company, being a friend,

but when I say no, I mean NO!
If you can't understand
with your ears maybe your shin,
groin, diaphragm or larynx will listen
to kicks, punches and piercing pain.

There are no limits to the ends
I will use to secure my sacredness.
I am High Priestess of my body.
I say who comes in or is left out
of places reserved for the devout.

No I don't really want it unless
I said yes and I don't care what
you think except if it is respect.
I own my body, power and sex.
I am not letting leases or releasing
my rights to decide, so accept

what comes next…
Getting your kicks may be more
than you planned. The ecstasy might
take you to new places on a scale of
holding cells and intensive care.

Be kind, respectful and fair…or beware.

Sounds and Silence

The voice was loud and shrill.
I could barely discern the words
"Get away, don't touch me!"
After a bang, the noise was followed
by a sudden silence.
I waited for the quiet to be broken by sirens.
They never came.
Stillness can be frightening.
A farmer I knew saved a baby rabbit
from thrashing combine blades,
but the little thing's spine was broken.
Until then I didn't know a bunny could scream.
It may not have shattered glass, but it
crumbled my heart into rough debris and dust.
How many women have suffered
at the hands of their savior?
How many apartment walls have shaken
with the sounds and silence?

Chrystine Julian

Thunderhead

She is stormy;
a thunderhead
coming across
a mountain pass
as an uncertain
threat at sunset,
the last laugh
of a bipolar day.

Her billowy
bold top glows,
touched with
pink and gold,
but beneath churns
a darkness
without molded
form.

We need the rain
but wonder
if it is worth
the boomers,
wind, whirls,
lightening,
emotional
cloud bursts
and soul erosion.

The Button

Nice dinner, the night is dressed to the nines.
Here happiness is served with fine silver and smiles.
Until she catches a glimpse of the gap in her shirt.

She'd checked it when she dressed,
but she can't seem to keep that damn button,
the one over her heart, sewn on.

There was no noise or notice when it popped off.
Though it is no surprise as it happened as it has before.
Especially sitting eye to eye with a person like this.

Was it the look she got or the one she gave
that caused her chest to swell with a breath too big?
If her feelings must be exposed, so it goes.

It is a night of social embarrassment.
"Oh God, don't let it be in the soup again."
she said beneath her breath.

The difference is she decides to leave it amiss.
There will be no pulling, pinning or covering up.
She'll pretend it is what she intended.

An observer might think her emotions
are inattentively attired, but the one with her now
enjoys the peek at her delicate cameo-soul.

It is the first step toward naked openness.
Tonight is more than a marvelous meal.
It is a meeting and merging of love.

When moved to uncover her inner self,
dinner is fine, but breakfast is divine.

Sort of Silly

Abstract Nonsense

pamper an amorous eloquent
carnivorous bowling ball

succulent yellow cellar door
natural cartoon wall

fundamental elemental
feline elephant

fellow elbow hysteria
hyper gentle galleon

luminous melancholy melody
savor relevant walleye quality

Chicken

I would write
poetry on poultry
but
I am just chicken

Weather Report

Weather report from space:
Dry and cold, and continued
cold through the weekend.
Air quality is Sucks, which
is normal in a near vacuum.
It is a lonely place, but
I enjoy the view.

Snake Dance

They said, "What a marvelous dance!
Look at him jump and prance!"
He replied, "No applause.
It is only because
A snake is up the leg of my pants!"

She betrayed a sly silent smile.
Then examined the wall's art deco style.
She dared not mention
Her secret intention.
After all, it was her pet reptile.

The crowd shifted, split and spread wide
As she quickly moved to his side.
She opened his belt,
Reached down and felt
All the places a boa might hide.

You see that is how it began.
They left walking hand in hand.
If her design doesn't falter
Soon they'll meet at the altar
Due to her sneaky snake plan.

Oops!

Oops can be the scariest
word in the world.
Especially when it is said
behind your head
by a stylist cutting
your hair or a chauffeur
winding you down
a narrow mountain
road.

An over tired pilot
bringing a plane in lightly,
Surgeon tying tubes or
chef concocting stew,
The man in charge of
locking cages at the zoo
Should all do their best
to be
oops averse
too.

Non Sequitur Nonsense

Illiterate alliteration
Malignant meter
Poetic power
Keyboard KPI

Prowling prowess
Languished language
Consistent consonance
Non sequitur nonsense

Chrystine Julian

Because Nothing Rhymes With Purple

Red had to interpolate
When purple ate her blues

Lazuli digested into azure means
She can sing only sanguine tunes

To her it is about balance
And modulating moods

Love

Love for Hire

Love for hire or love for higher expectations?
Love those that may never have opportunity to love you back
Love the unlovable
Love those that hate you
Treat others the way you want to be treated
These aren't others, only people we forgot
to invite to our economic party.

Quid Pro Quo

Unworthy, unworldly
Love

Wrapped in white
Light

Unlearning a quid pro quo
Quota

Tingly goose bump
Revelation

More sensation than
Manifestation

Being the feeling is
Believing

Sweet Silence

A boudoir offering
Humble and holy prayer

It begins with words and
Then ends beyond nothing

Whisper of wispy thoughts
Crystalline filigree

Delicately born beauty
Melting in monsoon love

Relevant intelligence
Drowned in sweet silence

Chocolate

In your hands
I am chocolate
on a summer day
softened and puddled
without form smeared
within the wrapper
messy, but still sweet
touch me with your tongue
lick me from the paper

Love Is a Flower

Cherry blossoms wake
A smile pollinates my heart
Love is a flower

Love stems push upward
Damp dark earth births light seekers
Buds become flowers

Love is a flower
Friends turn into a garden
Delight surrounds me

Natural Urge

Within the timber lives a red and amber
starving ember craving to caramelize air.

Beneath bark an embryo flame slumbers
like coiled thunder waiting to be sprung.

The flesh of my old growth soul feels
heat stirring and turning in restless sleep.

A natural urge, the dozing passion obsesses
on an opportune event of explosive expression.

Chrystine Julian

Tumbleweeds

Blown across the tan sand
and chaparral grass by
summer's charred winds
we tangle together as
the bristled thorns of two
tumbleweeds torn from
temporal youth and
shallow roots; sharp
and unattractive but
free and inseparable

Wonderfully Endless Thing

In the circle of the city square
A girl planted a magic seed.
It was a silly little whim.
The old folks grinned in sympathy.

She said it was a love seed
given to her by an old hag
that had passed the edge of town
giving out small bags.

She was told it would sprout
and spread wide into a giant tree
with fruits of love hanging low.
They only needed to wait and see.

The town folks hungered for love.
Little could be found because of drought.
They wanted such a thing to be true
but childish dreams do not pan out.

Each day the girl came with what water
she could find, then she'd tend and weed.
She spoke to anyone who listened about
how grand a tree of love would be.

Some say it was a miracle,
and that day the skeptics went mute,
in the city's center they awoke to find
a tree hanging with amorous fruit.

There was more than enough for everyone.
The people gathered, planning and
chattering while deciding what to do.
There was only one appropriate action.

They had to disburse the fruit,
let each person have two pieces.
They got one to pass along,
and then another one to keep.

If a piece was given to them,
they'd have two again.
So they repeated the process until
all but their one was given and gone.

The exchange goes on today.

They sing, in this a truth does ring,
love is a very magical, plentiful
wonderfully endless thing.

Packaged within these words
is a small bag with one seed.
I have grown up to be an old hag,
but stop me if you have a need…

for love.

Filigree

Your image is a filigree
heart delicately formed
by the alloy filaments
never to be forgotten

memories, fantasies
and empty feeling
trinket, bobble and fancy
beneath a fool's feet

Again

I don't understand
what I did
to deserve this
but if I did
I'd do it again
again
A look which
needs no words
to invite me in

Heartbeat

Heartbeat heartbeat heartbeat heartbeat
We meet
Hearts beat
So sweet
A need

Heartbeat heartbeat heartbeat heartbeat
High heat
Heartbeat
Complete
And neat

Heartbeat heartbeat heartbeat heartbeat
Bleeding
Heartbeat
Over
Leaving

Heartbeat heart-beat heart beat heart… beat
lonely
Bleep bleep
flat line
bleeeeeeep

Rights and Responsibilities

I Am Amazed

Our leaders are so smart that my
Insignificant intellect is shamed.

I have tried so hard but can't
Conjugate the way they do blame.

I am amazed.

In the wake of nine-eleven we invade
A country with boasts and ghosts of weapons

Then to the perpetrator's country of origin
Sell more state of the art munitions.

I am amazed.

Polarized priorities leave me shivering.
If my comprehension could expand

I'd warm in the comforts of manifest destiny.
If only my mind would stretch to understand

But I stay amazed.

Who I Am

Hey! Hey! Do you
understand who I am?

I am not a number or statistical anomaly,
not an unpronounceable nation from a fund raising occasion.
I live, breathe, love, hurt and heal
I am as human as you and important too.

Hey! Hey! Do you
understand who I am?

Drought may have left my tears dry, but the sound remains the
same.
Don't cover your ears or turn away your eyes.
The color of my skin is human. My religion is whichever deity will
feed me.
I reside everywhere… somehow. Have you noticed before now?

Hey! Hey! Do you
understand who I am?

I have a right to speak, be heard without needing to sneak around,
be treated with respect and that is what I expect.
Part of you dies when I bleed. My hunger is your own need.
Look at me and see your reality, your heart's story unfolding.

Hey! Hey! Do you
understand who I am?

We are all refugees from another place gathered in this existence.
We learn to huddle close for mutual protection. Only together will
we survive.
I'm not a stranger; I am your reflection in different clothes, but still
familiar.

Do you see that you and I are simply pieces, interlocking cutouts
of one species?

Hey! Hey! Do you
understand who I am?

Om Mani Padme Hum

Om Mani Padme Hum
Chenrezig, the Buddha that embodied compassion
I cry for your attention

There are some lessons in life that I wish were electives
Some text on which I'd rather not be tested
I want to wash the memories away, but only as
they remain can the world be moved to change

Om Mani Padme Hum
Chenrezig, the Buddha that embodied compassion
I cry for your attention

Chrystine Julian

What Do You Care

What do you care?

You don't know names.
They are bipedal skeleton figures
on an amateur landscape canvas.
No need to stare

What do you care?

Their voices speak
chatter instead of words
You know they'd stink
if you were there

What do you care?

All My Relations

Statistics are like stick figures.
They represent humans,
but nothing personal
until one of them takes on flesh
as a friend or family member
in a news flash. Then we empty
our cistern of tears
all brothers, all sisters.
If only we could know
all my relations.
Ho.

Ugly Field

An ugly field of weeds
grows where my garden
once bloomed and thrived
Some subterranean vermin
destroyed roots for feed
In much the way prophets
of intolerance take away
distorted need or greed
The life, colors and scents
Of "different" people being free
I miss the nosegay array of
eye catching reds mingled
with purples, yellows and blues

America the Unattractive - July 4, 2008

Patriotic songs seem odd to me today.
Somebody somewhere said that beauty
is skin deep, but ugly goes to the core.

America, America, God repoed his grace,
dethroned our good and declared us
the dishonored home for homely souls.

Heartless in the heartland, besieged
by muggy summer rain and heat,
no brotherhood crown in the hood.

I was not there in Wichita, but I have
to wonder what the hell happened.
Isn't that that part of the fruited plains?

In a busy C-store a woman lay
bleeding from a stabbing wound,
and rather than calling for help

Someone used their camera phone
to take her picture, stepped on to pay
for beer and then left… I don't get it.

We proclaim godly values, but imitate
the holy men that pass by on the other side.
Instead of Americans we need Samaritans.

Some folks in central Texas beat and kill
a passenger from an automobile altercation
and a hate crime victim dives to his death.

We hold these truths to be self-evident, that
all people are created, but not treated equal
in a country where freedoms are only falsies.

We dress in red, white and blue to promenade
in a pageant of self-proclaimed pretty people,
but bulges rip the seams of our spangled gown.

Even thick concealer cannot cover our blemishes.
We look like clowns instead of crowned by God
beauty queens and spokes models for the world.

I am not attracted to the image in this mirror.
I have to question if maybe it is time to create
Extreme Makeover, the country edition.

Defamation

Character assassination
Hurled on a race
Particular place
Origin or religion

Devaluing one
Defames and
Degrades all

Desecration
In a fit of evaluation
Is a misplaced
Uniting lace
Of human evolution

Alchemy

Gold from lead
Truth from lies
What the man said left
Tens of thousands lying

bA3b in a pool of reflection

There is so little
Belief in magic lingering
The dog and pony show leaves
Us to clean the mess of litter

Magi fallen short of perfection

Some Sing for Joy

Some sing for joy,
I pray for tears
because we are closer
during crying.
Prosperity wishes leave us
empty and hopeless
when holding a child dying.
Bursting compassion's
dam looses floods
of feelings
that fill us with love.
I looked at the world today,
and cried.

Chrystine Julian

Fringe

I live on the fringe
tugging at the threads of society
unnerving a few folks
that are using it as a parachute
I unravel the fabric
the economic elite establishment
has a long way to fall

People, Places and Things

Parking Lot Performers

It was just a required spot of greenery, a parking lot landscape provision meant to be ignored except in a sketch.

Did the planners include birds like the yellow-green breasted family who found refuge and a playground?

Were architect's drawings only black and white number two pencil or did they understand a mix of burnt red, yellow and orange in a time of change?

Young trees put on their best show, but remain unnoticed and uncompensated street performers and shopping cart stoppers.

Perhaps it is a shame that there is little appreciation for the beauty and art springing up around us.

Benazir Bhutto

I heard her speak in person – Bakersfield, CA,
beneath a tent with five-thousand.
Her scarf was light; every few seconds she
would pull it back to its proper position

She spoke about power and respect for women,
about democracy, military coup d'état
and modernization of ancient society;
a gentle voice in a violent world

A violent world that hushes the gentle
when it sounds too loud, reverberating,
shaking and threatening the stone
of their so-called hearts.

The Party Is Over

Our trees were serious celebrants.

They pranced in pompous festive garb,
dancing with the wind
late in the season
until exhaustion overtook them.

In the end,
they dropped their clothes
and fell asleep where they stood.

Resurrection Day

An annual celebration of a special occasion set in motion by the shy retreat of insecure, neurotic and unmediated short fall daylight shivering under a blanket of night.

Ritual candle flames dance and flicker within their container as hot chocolate and cookies wait to consummate communion.

It is a reunion much like friends remembering and regretting circumstances beyond control that drove them into separation and seclusion.

Resurrection done by shaking back to life sweaters, mittens, knitted woolen scarves and other embodiments of cuddly clothing entombed within a cedar sarcophagus.

Cloudy Day

I take comfort in a cloudy day
putting on a cherished sweater
for the first time each year

It is not pretty, just very cozy
We have shared good times
and opportunities for tears

I Am Ready

I am ready
To put up
My sandals and
Pull out the
Flannels and fleece
Stunted shorter than average days
Suffering from early onset
Sleepiness and cuddling up ways

Space is a Lonely Place

Space is a lonely place so I decided to check out the neighborhood cabaret.

A mirror ball turns and a saxophone moans melodic sounds of sensual pleasure.
Speckled lights adorn the black velvet back curtain and inside roof of the stage.

The moon strips off her strapless evening gown and dances naked across the ceiling.
Men stare intently and become engorged with the universal and fantastical lunacy.

Adoration of the masses is incidental and insignificant to her romantic resolution.
She pays them little regard, the come hither motion is designed to entice the tide.

It has been eons since the ocean rejected, ejected and sent her to orbit in the cold.
She watches the waterline realizing he is reaching and knowing they cannot connect.

Acquiescing to being briefly alluring and capturing attention for a few hours of honor,
She reconciles to understanding that desire is demanding and fulfillment is disaster.

As lights come up she fades away without waiting for applause or tips from the audience.

Untimely Passing

I am accosted by news of a friend's untimely passing.

Here it comes again, a boot to the head, knee to the groin and piercing heart sting that doubles me over as my spine dissolves in tears.

Death is a vagrant but vigilant mugger springing on the vulnerable from an alley shadow blind.

He enjoys rolling drunken revelers in immortality illusions and leaving them as paupers reeling in pain.

I avoid unlit avenues, but he sits in silence enumerating steps until at the opening he can stretch forth and snag my sense of security.

He drags me into the darkness camouflaged form and then muffles the struggle for my emotions until my sense of serenity is left for dead.

Chrystine Julian

Drum Circle Heaven

Will there be a drum circle heaven?

Will it be unbroken in the sky?
Will they play a backbeat rhythm?
Pounded out in three-four time?

I've seen a glimpse of drum circle heaven.

Divine intervention in many towns
When my friends gather friends around
and start the djembe and djun-djun sounds.

If there is a drum circle heaven

Perhaps St. Peter picks up an a-go-go
Wooden frog or a dumbek made of gold
facilitating in a style stolen from Arthur Hull.

If there is no drum circle heaven

There is no need to save my soul
Cause, I won't want or plead to go.
I'll just do a stop then fade on a roll.

I Have a Drum

I have a drum boom-ba-dum

While playing I perceive
the heartbeat of the world

I have a drum boom-ba-dum

And in that space all people
are equal in speech and song

I have a drum boom-ba-dum

Where sonic strands weave into
a gossamer and satin sound

I have a drum boom-ba-dum

A blanket wrapping divided souls
in elegance, solace and warmth

I have a drum boom-ba-dum

A pebble plopped into a pond
and resonating circle ripples

I have a drum boom-ba-dum

Chrystine Julian

Where rebels against hate
and bureaucracy congregate

I have a drum boom-ba-dum

Making waves that touch
things beyond my myopia

I have a drum boom-ba-dum

A space for love as metaphor
the rhythm of throbbing hearts

I have a drum

Hero's Holiday

Gather and allow songs to levitate across empty spaces
Stretch up onto your toes and pirouette together
Fall completes a death march with festivities

Understand that when night reaches its longest stay
Then, only then will light start to slowly grow
It is the holy hallowing of the year's shortest day

There are many reasons for celebration
Mother Earth and Father Sky are consummating their marriage
It is the orgasmic origin of winter's burgeoning gestation

Blood starts pumping through an embryo season
Until, when fully formed the champion springs
From the womb proclaiming renewal

Maturing to become the hero that saddles the sun
He rides the range of summer sky on the brilliant horse
To provision us with the spoils of harvest

And then in turn parades in pompous colors
To surrender his passionate life at the gate of fate
In exchange for a promissory note of rebirth

Mother and father cuddle close for comfort
Against the chills of evening and grief
Within their intimacy the cycle again begins

Gather and allow songs to levitate across empty spaces
Stretch up onto your toes and pirouette together
Revel in the hero's holiday

Chrystine Julian

Darkest Day of the Year

Upon occasion I find artifacts
When groping about in dim lit corners.
Perhaps some super race once occupied
These deeply shadowed abiding quarters

What may be a discard-able tool or
Bobble becomes hope and inspiration
When slithering to a drain and being
Sucked through a pipeline of ascension

Christmas Tree Empathy

She looked at the discarded tree
lying by the walk.
She cried
from a deep sadness
inside her understanding.

It had been beautiful,
full height but still young.
It was cut away
from its family,
taken in and kept warm.

He spent a small fortune
decorating it for show,
but when his pleasure ended,
it was tossed nearly naked
into the snow.

She cries because
she knows how that feels.

Spirit

Chrystine Julian

Whisper

For the butterfly to emerge
a caterpillar must surrender

For the cherries to come
blossoms drop and wither

Listen to their lessons
lean into the whisper

Come

Come!

We are waiting
Bring your laughter
Join our dance
The song is never complete
Without the music
Your heart makes

Dance!

Remember the moves
Your body knows
So does your soul
Surrender to movement
Love in motion
Invoke, evoke and emote

Love!

There is no forgetting
No dementia to diminish
Performance of passion
Remember the rapture
Your first lover
Your first breath

Breathe!

Simple breathing
Empty chest
Unburden heart
Push it out and
In flows the fresh
Fill, release and repeat

Flow!

The universe moves
Swirling around
And moving beyond
Let it take you
Bring you
To this place

Come!

Ripe and Rotten

Thin separation between ripe and rotten

Reality and realms of pungent passion

Perfect progression to release the seeds

Chrystine Julian

Let the Beauty Be Love

Be
what we do

There are hundreds of ways
in which to pray

Kneel beside a garden row

Sing a song,
or dance along

Smile at a small child

Allow glistening eyes
to touch a passerby

Let them see you

Be a star in the night
Someone's guiding light

Be what we do

There are hundreds of ways
in which to pray

Better

She said, "Better! Be better!"
I insisted, "Never...ever!"

Better is always somewhere a here beyond where I am.

Better is a place of if, when and then another better off is still beyond

I can be only now, as is, no guarantee or warranty.

Like good leather, imperfections are marks of individualization.

I prefer being with beautiful beings over needing to be better.

Devotion

Humble home early morn devotion and prayer
Mat meticulously placed for a forehead's rest
Incense invisibly washing worries from the air
Brass bowl vibrations under a caressing dowel

Holy honey for the bitterness of a cold society
Many the mantras for a mingled mangled mind
Inventing innocent manifestations of empathy
Beg beauty, pray peace and cry for compassion

Names

I take no pride or disgrace
by way of names or titles:
called bright, generous and creative
and occasionally LFD (late for dinner).

They label me old, fat, ugly and stupid,
beautiful, shaman, healer and teacher,
forgotten lover and annoyer, drummer,
dancer, prophet, and/or poet.

My real name is silent presence, which
is the only calling to which I will answer.

Chrystine Julian

Short Changed

When a best friend becomes bested fiend

Small changes leave me short changed

That which is seen is not as it seemed

An endless search for a meaningful end

Morning Star

I like listening to conversations
even if the speakers don't see me.

While eavesdropping on the day
I saw the morning star peeking

from between the branches. She
was scouting for a place to party.

Then I heard her call back to the sun,
Hurry! Come! Hurry, hurry!

They are waiting for you.
All they need is your awakening

and invitation for them to dance.
This may be a gathering

that I need to crash.

Complete

When life is complete carry the stiff body

To be buried overlooking the mystic city

Where reality is myth and dreams endure

Secured tightly in a vault of vulnerability

God Called Me to His Office

It was after hours.

God called me to his corner office on the top most floor.

I was fearful of being punished for selfishness and an assortment of other sins.

But God was on a bender.

He only laughed, danced and flaunted a collection of rare and beautiful things.

Then came the seduction.

It started with a kiss; a full on deep probing of my darkest cavities.

I willingly opened.

We became intimate to the point of losing sensations of separation.

I could tell more details.

Perhaps it is enough to know God calls only when he wants to make love.

Chrystine Julian

A Heart Filled with Mercy

A heart filled with mercy is a well full of strength
Buckets dip spilling forgiveness on parched earth
Trickle after trickle build to a river of compassion

I pray we be washed and carried away in the flood
Tear down false securities and facades of failings
Let us live, flowing freely, a shoreless sea of love

The Dreamer

I am a dream.
The one I love
is the dreamer.

Awakening's
astringent nature
dissolves all.

But the mind
of the dreamer
remembers.

Then I exist
as a wisp
within the one.

Chrystine Julian

Empty

My thoughts MT

A shoulder feels narrow and weak without your leaning
head

My thoughts MT

A hand lacks strength when delicate fingers untwine

My thoughts MT

Daydreams wander pointlessly in a vacant lot

My thoughts MT

At dawn daylight sketches and etches shadows

My thoughts MT

Until the sun sets into a clouded shroud

And my thoughts again empty

Thirst

I stagger in thirst and fall on the beach
of an ocean from which I cannot drink.

Salted water is not fit for my consumption.

I inquire of a passing fish what it is like
to have no limit on what he may gulp.

He knows nothing regarding bodies of water.

How can it be that you live in this vast
mass of liquid and never have to swallow?

My desire is to lose parched love.

I know naught of what you call sea,
all about me is what I breathe.

Die Before I Die

Let my life of greed die
Die before I die
Let my life of need die
Afterlife after dying
Here and now always smiling

Nothing Is More Precious to Me

Songs become quiet memories.
Movement of dancing stops.
Then my room starts spinning.

That is when you cocoon me

In your silk sleeved embrace.
Among all of this life's jewels,
Nothing is more precious to me.

Chrystine Julian

Being Beneath the Being

Speaking of soul is cliché,
vulgar, and perhaps passé

So I'll write that my being beneath
the being of tactual experience

Unwed consciousness holding hands and
cuddling with a flame while cohabiting my flesh

When freed will scour humbly
in a wild scavenger hunt

For the brilliant scattered glitter
of gilded but broken connectors

Previous passion and persistent recollection
of dearly departed day dreamed rapture

That essence is looking to reassemble
a semblance of personal worth

A sustaining substance beyond words
and the world order of ordinary

Revised edition convictions and fictions
of morality subverted urges

Be Buzzes

Beneath my Bodhi tree
Be buzzes turn to stings
Believing has no meanings

Because to me
Being is sanctification
Beyond ordeal ordained salvation

Temple

My physique is a temple dome
of descended holy presence,
with no worshipers or devotees.
Had a choice been given
I would have preferred it be
a tavern with glory and angels
singing, laughing, dancing and
matching up for making love.

My Body

My body is stretched
over a frame of light
and stapled into place

As a canvas for a modern
abstract by the divine
master artist of creation

If you see me smiling
it is only because some
times the brush tickles

Chrystine Julian

Do Over

With a chance to live again
I would change everything

I'd value bravery over morality
castrate the core of my fears

Perhaps remember the weather
on a first day shopping together

Priorities would be on more
encounters of carnal pleasures

Make notes on how the sun
warmly massaged my skin

Or the rush of cold air sliding
up my nose and down my throat

I'd skip the danish and doughnuts
eating only the fruit bowl

Ecstasy

Ecstasy, insanity,
drunkenness and drowning
are metaphors
of effects, influence and
desires for divinity
with good reason
beyond rational reality
Umm… how sweet it is.

What Is Is

Not what is bad
Or what is good
Nothing is right

Nonexistent
Punishable
Altercation

All is measure
of what is or
is not real love

Alone

Chrystine Julian

From the Shadows

Did you know I loved you?
Could you tell? Did you care?
Would you say it's nothing new
because so many others stare?

Do they know your favorite pizza
or where you buy those shoes?
Would they light up just to see ya?
Are you called their major muse?

I sit silently watching from a shadow
beneath a caped black cloak of fear
and in a sty of loneliness I wallow
too self aware to dare come near.

Did they tell you of my passing
or where my body is laid to rot?
Will any love thoughts be lasting?
More than likely, they will not.

Decades Meld

Decades meld while
I am watching the
Moody Blues on YouTube

In boredom I play poker
with a pinochle deck
I keep getting great hands

but never come out ahead
I spill Scrabble squares
on a Monopoly board

and attempt finding sense
in the intellectual property
values of incomplete words

Chrystine Julian

Home Alone

Home alone
Reminiscing
While reading
Poems by Rumi

Ancient tones
Resonating
Until meaning
Comes to me

Sensual Spirit...poetry and thoughts from the place where body and soul mee, by Chrystine Julian. "What a rapturous book! Chrystine Julian weds wit and wisdom, body and spirit, in these poems. Her warmth and humor and deep insight radiate off every page." *Gayle Brandeis, author of "Fruitflesh, Seeds of Inspiration for Women that Write," "Self Storage" and the Bellwether Prize winner, "The Book of Dead Birds."*

Pawprints by Ina Hillebrandt, Amazon.com top seller featured on ABC Nightly News, PBS, etc. From "Moonlit Fox" to "Nose Fur," more than 100 short, short "tails" of close encounters of the furry kind. Uplifts, inspires readers to write, and promotes kindness to animals. Purr-fect gift for animal lovers and pets of all ages. "The stories make you feel you are right there...I love them!" Teresa Proscewitz, Chief Forester, City of LA Dept. of Recreation and Parks. ISBN 1-880882-01-9.

The Student Prints, Educators' Guide to Pawprints Literacy Plus™ —The Innovative Standards-Based Literacy and Environmental Program. © 2001 Ina S. Hillebrandt. Companion curriculum guide to *Pawprints*, developed following Pawprints Literacy Plus training module for Jane Goodall Institute. For teachers and parents, grades 1-8, and ESL. "*Pawprints* is a new form of great literature...the book and these exercises have the power to change the way kids...and...adults think." Maxwell Yerger, Reading Specialist/Teacher/Trainer, NY,NY. ISBN 1-880882–03-5.

How to Write Your Memoirs — Fun Prompts to Make Writing ... and Reading ...Your Life Stories a Pleasure! by Ina Hillebrandt. Easy steps and prompts to make organizing those scraps of paper — physical and mental — fun and rewarding, for the writer, family and friends, and possibly, the public! ISBN 1-880882-04-3. *"The questions make it easy!" Gertrude Brucker, Member, Felicia Mahood Senior Center, Los Angeles*

Stories From The Heart, Volumes 1-3 ... Selected stories to delight and inspire readers to create their own memoirs and fiction. Vol. 3 Includes writing tools and carefully selected memoirs -- and fiction! -- to entertain, and help readers craft their own enchanting life histories. *"Multi-hued, textured tales – from such stuff was woven the American Dream." Marvin J. Wolf, Author of Fallen Angels and many other nonfiction books.*

Vol. 2, From great grape fiascos to wars...Wit and wisdom by the Pawprints Writing Club (now Footprints) became an **Amazon.com top seller**. Poignant, funny, tender, frightening, insightful memories of the holocaust, flying a plane, bees, first love, South Africa, India in the time of the Raj, cookies and much more. *"The section I most enjoyed was a few punning stories about cats by the late Earl Boretz...most amusing. His characters include Count Fe-Line the cat burglar in Pussy footin' around; Sinister, the three-legged pirate cat and Sorrowful, the witch...Overall, an entertaining collection."* Cecilia Blight, *Nelm News, newsletter of The* **National English Literary Museum**, *Grahamstown, S. Africa.*

    Vol. 1 features the first delightful tails by Earl Boretz, plus the special whimsy of Arabella Bel-Mitchell, a British lady with an outrageous sense of humor and fantasy, along with lyrical and heartfelt memoirs by authors from various walks of life.

All three **Stories** books compiled and edited by Ina Hillebrandt. Vol. 1 ISBN. 1-880882-07-8. Vol. 2 ISBN 1-880882-08-6 Vol. 3 ISBN 1-80882-04-3.

Go East, Young Man, Go East! Memoirs of an eyewitness to the oil boom and culture clashes of the Middle East. By Charles Alan Tichenor, Edited by Ina Hillebrandt. A book of memoirs penned by a witty and informed hand, with tales of political intrigue, spies, cultural exchanges and the effects of black gold on royalty and desert-dwelling Bedouins. ISBN 1-880882-09-4.

Edited by Ina Hillebrandt, Published by Angel Fire Publications

The Angel Chronicles, by J.K. Johnson. A compelling murder mystery/ romance with feet in this world and another plane. Written originally from behind prison bars, this page turner by a multi talented woman inspires readers to say, "It's a life changer! And a great read." ISBN 978-0-9819193-0-0.

To order any of our books, please visit Amazon.com or your local bookstore. **Also available: writing workshops and coaching by Ina**. For more information, and for bulk orders, please visit our website, http://www.InasPawprints.com.

Percussion as Poetry

A CD with the passion of Chrystine's poetry expressed by rhythmic voices of instruments from around the world

Available at iTunes, Amazon.com and other digital music download sites

Chrystine Julian is a poet, mystic, musician, drummer, drum circle facilitator and workshop leader.

Her programs include:

Team – Tribe
Team Building with rhythm

Talking Your Power
Put your power where your mouth is.

Sacred Space Community Dances
Sacred ceremony in dance

Sex and the Shaman
Recapturing our bodies and power

She can also be found performing and reading her poetry at various venues around Southern California.

Information is available at

ChrystineDrums.com

e-mail: LadyLovesDrums@aol.com

www.ingramcontent.com/pod-product-compliance
Lightning Source LLC
Chambersburg PA
CBHW060949050726
47592CB00003B/1173